EXPLORING THE STATES

Indiana

THE HOOSIER STATE

by Pat Ryan

BELLWETHER MEDIA • MINNEAPOLIS, MN

Note to Librarians, Teachers, and Parents:

Blastoff! Readers are carefully developed by literacy experts and combine standards-based content with developmentally appropriate text.

Level 1 provides the most support through repetition of high-frequency words, light text, predictable sentence patterns, and strong visual support.

Level 2 offers early readers a bit more challenge through varied simple sentences, increased text load, and less repetition of high-frequency words.

Level 3 advances early-fluent readers toward fluency through increased text and concept load, less reliance on visuals, longer sentences, and more literary language.

Level 4 builds reading stamina by providing more text per page, increased use of punctuation, greater variation in sentence patterns, and increasingly challenging vocabulary.

Level 5 encourages children to move from "learning to read" to "reading to learn" by providing even more text, varied writing styles, and less familiar topics.

Whichever book is right for your reader, Blastoff! Readers are the perfect books to build confidence and encourage a love of reading that will last a lifetime!

This edition first published in 2014 by Bellwether Media, Inc.

No part of this publication may be reproduced in whole or in part without written permission of the publisher. For information regarding permission, write to Bellwether Media, Inc., Attention: Permissions Department, 5357 Penn Avenue South, Minneapolis, MN 55419.

Library of Congress Cataloging-in-Publication Data

Ryan, Patrick, 1948-
Indiana / by Pat Ryan.
    pages cm. – (Blastoff! readers. Exploring the states)
Includes bibliographical references and index.
Summary: "Developed by literacy experts for students in grades three through seven, this book introduces young readers to the geography and culture of Indiana"– Provided by publisher.
ISBN 978-1-62617-013-1 (hardcover : alk. paper)
1. Indiana–Juvenile literature. I. Title.
F526.3.R93 2014
977.2–dc23

2013002419

Printed in the United States of America, North Mankato, MN.

Table of Contents

Where Is Indiana?   4
History   6
The Land   8
Limestone Caves   10
Wildlife   12
Landmarks   14
Indianapolis   16
Working   18
Playing   20
Food   22
Festivals   24
Circus City   26
Fast Facts   28
Glossary   30
To Learn More   31
Index   32

Where Is Indiana?

Indiana lies near the center of the United States. Covering 36,417 square miles (94,320 square kilometers), it is the smallest state in the **Midwest**. Modern highways, railroads, and waterways crisscross the state. These inspired the state motto, "The Crossroads of America."

The northwestern corner of Indiana touches Lake Michigan. The state of Michigan lies to the north. To the east is Ohio, and to the west is Illinois. Across the Ohio River to the south is Kentucky. The state capital of Indianapolis is located in the center of the state.

Illinois

fun fact

Indiana is nicknamed the Hoosier State. No one knows the real reason for the name. Some say it comes from the Indiana way of greeting strangers by asking, "Who's here?"

Lake Michigan

Michigan

South Bend

Fort Wayne

Ohio

Indiana

Indianapolis

Marengo Cave
Wyandotte Cave

Ohio River

Evansville

N
W E
S

Kentucky

History

Indiana means "land of the Indians." The first **native** peoples lived there more than 10,000 years ago. Europeans arrived in 1679. French traders came for beaver, mink, and other valuable furs. The British later gained control of the area. After the **Revolutionary War**, Indiana became part of the United States. It was granted statehood in 1816.

fur trading

Indiana Timeline!

1679:	French explorer René-Robert Cavelier arrives in what is now northern Indiana.
1763:	The British take over the land at the end of the French and Indian War.
1783:	The Revolutionary War ends. The United States gains land that includes Indiana.
1800:	The Indiana Territory is created.
1811:	The Battle of Tippecanoe takes place. William Henry Harrison defeats several Native American tribes in a fight over Indiana land.
1816:	Indiana becomes the nineteenth state.
1825:	Indianapolis becomes the state capital.
1861–1865:	Indiana and other northern states fight against the southern states in the American Civil War.
1911:	The first Indianapolis 500 race takes place.

René-Robert Cavelier

Battle of Tippecanoe

first Indianapolis 500

The Land

Ohio River

Indiana has three rich and **diverse** land regions. The Great Lakes **Plains** cover the northern part of the state. Their **fertile** soil makes good farmland. **Glaciers** left behind many small lakes and hills in the area. The Till Plains are in the center of the state. These lands are also good for farming.

Indiana's Climate
average °F

spring
Low: 41°
High: 62°

summer
Low: 63°
High: 84°

fall
Low: 44°
High: 64°

winter
Low: 21°
High: 37°

The plains give way to the Southern Hills and Lowlands. This is the only part of the state that the glaciers did not grind down. Southern Indiana is a wonderland of streams and limestone caves. Indiana has snowy winters and hot summers. Storms are common in spring. Indianans enjoy beautiful fall colors.

Limestone Caves

Wyandotte Cave of southern Indiana boasts some of the largest underground spaces in the country. The limestone was worn away by underground rivers. This left miles of tunnels. The cave is so large that it has a mountain inside of it! At 175 feet (53 meters) high, Monument Mountain is the largest underground mountain in the world.

Nearby Marengo Cave was found by local children in 1883. The owner of the land explored the cave and made it a **tourist** attraction. This cave has an underground waterfall. It also features **stalactites**, **stalagmites**, and formations that look like curtains and popcorn.

Bats are just some of the shy animals that can be found in the hidden places of Indiana. White-tailed deer were once almost **extinct** in the state. Now they bound through the forests and farmland. Foxes, rabbits, and raccoons can be found throughout Indiana. North America's only **marsupial**, the opossum, is also common.

Birds fill Indiana's skies. Bald eagles can be spotted in trees along the rivers and lakes. Ruffed grouse, swifts, and wild turkeys are found in the woods. Indiana's waters are home to many kinds of fish. Bass, trout, and salmon swim in the cool rivers and lakes.

opossum

bald eagle

wild turkey

white-tailed deer

13

fun fact

The Indianapolis Motor Speedway was paved with more than 3 million bricks. Only a narrow strip of them remains uncovered. Winners of the Indianapolis 500 celebrate by kissing the bricks.

The Indianapolis Motor Speedway is the state's most famous landmark. It is the home of the Indianapolis 500. Around 400,000 people attend the event each May. Colorful race cars zoom around the track at more than 200 miles (320 kilometers) per hour. The speedway's Hall of Fame Museum has a collection of more than 30 winning cars.

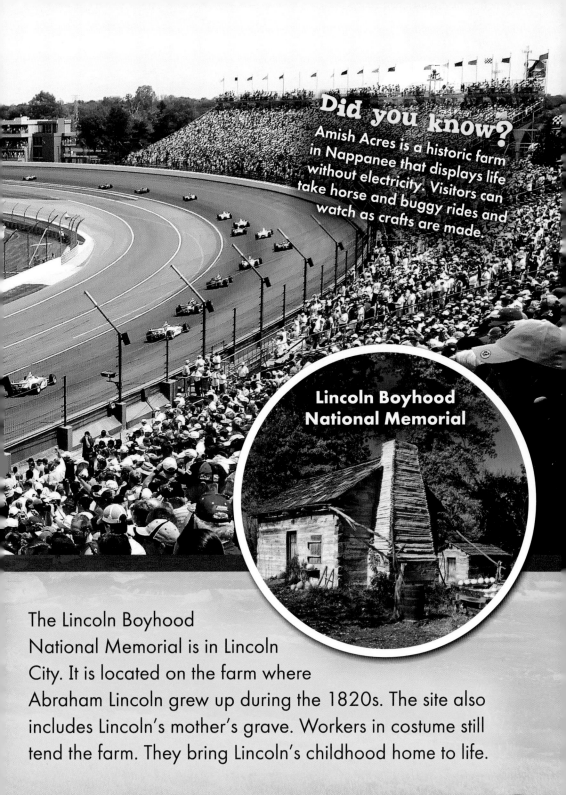

Did you know?
Amish Acres is a historic farm in Nappanee that displays life without electricity. Visitors can take horse and buggy rides and watch as crafts are made.

Lincoln Boyhood National Memorial

The Lincoln Boyhood National Memorial is in Lincoln City. It is located on the farm where Abraham Lincoln grew up during the 1820s. The site also includes Lincoln's mother's grave. Workers in costume still tend the farm. They bring Lincoln's childhood home to life.

Indianapolis

Indianapolis is the capital city of Indiana. It was founded in 1821 almost exactly in the center of the state. With a population of 820,445, it is also the state's largest city. Indianapolis has a thriving downtown area with many shops, restaurants, and museums.

Monument Circle lies at the heart of the city. Its 285-foot (87-meter) monument honors Indiana's soldiers and sailors. The Indianapolis Symphony Orchestra plays at the Hilbert Circle Theatre. Indianapolis is also home to winning sports teams. Fans follow the Colts football and Pacers basketball teams.

Peyton Manning

fun fact

The Indianapolis Colts have been to four Super Bowls. They won in 2007 thanks to quarterback Peyton Manning. The 2012 Super Bowl was held in Indianapolis.

**Monument
Circle**

Indianans work a wide variety of jobs. Farmland covers most of the state. Corn and soybeans are the most important crops. Some of the corn is used to make **ethanol**. Workers dig for coal in southwestern Indiana. Coal is another source of energy.

Factory workers in large cities make medicines, steel, and transportation equipment. These products are shipped to other states and countries. Many Indianans have **service jobs**. They work in banks, hospitals, stores, and restaurants.

fun fact

From 1900 to 1920, more than 200 makes of cars were produced in the Hoosier State.

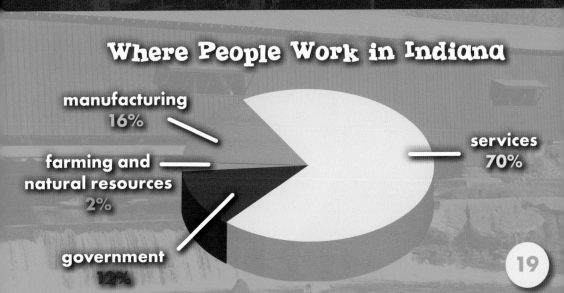

Where People Work in Indiana

manufacturing
16%

farming and natural resources
2%

government
12%

services
70%

Playing

Indianans are crazy about basketball. The high school tournament is a popular event. Each year, people follow the dreams of boys and girls as they compete. Many of these young players go on to become professionals. Football fans follow the Notre Dame Fighting Irish, the Purdue Boilermakers, and the Indiana Hoosiers. The stadiums are filled with loyal supporters on Saturday afternoons.

The people of Indiana are also active outdoors. They enjoy biking, running, and water sports. On the weekends they explore state parks. They also tour the state's museums and historic sites.

fun fact

Some of the greatest professional basketball players have come from Indiana. Oscar Robertson and Larry Bird are both in the NBA Hall of Fame.

Sugar Cream Pie
(Hoosier Pie)

Ingredients:

- 1 (9 inch) pie crust, baked
- 4 tablespoons cornstarch
- 3/4 cup white sugar
- 6 tablespoons butter, melted
- 2 1/4 cups half & half cream
- 1 teaspoon vanilla extract
- 1/2 teaspoon ground cinnamon

Directions:

1. Mix cornstarch and sugar. Add 4 tablespoons butter and half & half.

2. Cook over medium heat, stirring constantly, until mixture boils and becomes thick and creamy. Remove from heat and stir in the vanilla.

3. Preheat oven broiler to high.

4. Pour mixture into piecrust. Drizzle 2 tablespoons butter over top and sprinkle with cinnamon.

5. Put under broiler until butter bubbles. It doesn't take long, so watch it carefully.

6. Refrigerate for at least 1 hour before serving.

pork tenderloin sandwich

Indiana kitchens are full of rich, hearty foods. The pork tenderloin sandwich is a Hoosier classic. A large piece of pork is breaded, fried, and served on a toasted bun. Fresh-baked rolls and biscuits go well with chili, onion pie, and other satisfying dishes.

The **Amish** people of Indiana also influence the state's food. They make an apple butter spread with slow-cooked apples and spices. Their pies also contribute to Indiana's sweet tooth. Shoofly pie is a favorite dessert made with molasses. Indiana's state pie is the sugar cream pie. This simple dessert is flavored with butter, cream, vanilla, and sugar.

Festivals

Many of Indiana's small towns host food festivals. Valparaiso's Popcorn Festival takes place every September. The event features a parade, arts and crafts, and plenty of popcorn. Along with blueberry dishes, the Marshall County Blueberry Festival has fireworks and a car show.

Every July, the Indiana Black Expo stages its Summer Celebration in Indianapolis. This event honors the contributions African Americans have made to Indiana and the world. Columbus hosts the **Ethnic** Expo to celebrate Indiana's diversity. The two-day festival features ethnic foods, music and dancing, and an international market.

Indiana Black Expo

! fun fact

The 500 Festival boasts one of the largest parades in the nation. Thousands of people line the streets of the capital to celebrate the Indianapolis 500.

500 Festival parade

25

Circus City

The people of Peru, Indiana, have the circus in their blood. Benjamin Wallace brought the first circus to the city in the 1880s. The Ringling Brothers and other traveling circuses spent their winters in Peru. Today, the International Circus Hall of Fame stands on the old circus grounds.

Every year, more than 200 young people perform in the Peru **Amateur** Circus. They become jugglers, tightrope walkers, **trapeze** flyers, and clowns. This spectacular show always draws a crowd. Some participants go on to careers with the circus. Indiana's fun history lives on in Circus City and throughout the Hoosier State.

Fast Facts About Indiana

Indiana's Flag

Indiana's flag is deep blue with two circles of gold stars. The stars show that Indiana was the nineteenth state to join the Union. The outer stars stand for the first thirteen colonies. The largest star stands for Indiana. Underneath it is a golden torch with a sparkling flame for freedom.

State Flower
peony

State Nickname:	Hoosier State
State Motto:	"The Crossroads of America"
Year of Statehood:	1816
Capital City:	Indianapolis
Other Major Cities:	Fort Wayne, Evansville, South Bend
Population:	6,483,802 (2010)
Area:	36,417 square miles (94,320 square kilometers); Indiana is the 38th largest state.
Major Industries:	farming, manufacturing, mining
Natural Resources:	limestone, coal, oil, natural gas
State Government:	100 representatives; 50 senators
Federal Government:	9 representatives; 2 senators
Electoral Votes:	11

State Bird
northern cardinal

Glossary

amateur—one who practices a certain activity but is not a professional

Amish—a religious group whose beliefs prevent them from using modern technology such as cars and electricity

diverse—made up of many different types or coming from many different backgrounds

ethanol—a type of fuel that is made from corn

ethnic—from another country or cultural background

extinct—no longer living

fertile—able to support growth

glaciers—massive sheets of ice that cover large areas of land

marsupial—an animal that carries its young in a pouch attached to the belly

Midwest—a region of 12 states in the north-central United States

monument—a structure that people build to remember important events or people

native—originally from a specific place

plains—large areas of flat land

Revolutionary War—the war between 1775 and 1783 in which the United States fought for independence from Great Britain

service jobs—jobs that perform tasks for people or businesses

stalactites—icicle-shaped formations that hang from a cave's ceiling

stalagmites—cone-shaped formations that rise from a cave's floor

tourist—someone who travels to visit another place

trapeze—a swing from which circus performers hang

To Learn More

AT THE LIBRARY

Downey, Tika. *Indiana: The Hoosier State*. New York, N.Y.: PowerKids Press, 2010.

Hamilton, S. L. *Indianapolis 500*. Minneapolis, Minn.: ABDO Publishing, 2013.

Ling, Bettina. *Indiana*. New York, N.Y.: Children's Press, 2009.

ON THE WEB

Learning more about Indiana is as easy as 1, 2, 3.

1. Go to www.factsurfer.com.

2. Enter "Indiana" into the search box.

3. Click the "Surf" button and you will see a list of related Web sites.

With factsurfer.com, finding more information is just a click away.

Index

500 Festival, 25

activities, 20

Amish, 15, 23

capital (see Indianapolis)

circus, 26-27

climate, 9

Ethnic Expo, 24

festivals, 24-25

food, 22-23

history, 6-7, 27

Indiana Black Expo, 24

Indianapolis, 4, 5, 7, 14, 16-17, 24, 25

Indianapolis 500, 7, 14, 25

Indianapolis Motor Speedway, 14

International Circus Hall of Fame, 26

landmarks, 14-15

landscape, 8-11

limestone caves, 9, 10-11

Lincoln Boyhood National Memorial, 15

location, 4-5

Marengo Cave, 5, 10

Marshall County Blueberry Festival, 24

Monument Circle, 16, 17

Peru Amateur Circus, 27

Popcorn Festival, 24

sports, 16, 20, 21

wildlife, 12-13

working, 18-19

Wyandotte Cave, 5, 10, 11

The images in this book are reproduced through the courtesy of: Jason Titzer, front cover (bottom); Akg-images/ Newscom, p. 6; Niday Picture Library/ Alamy, p. 7 (left); (Collection)/ Prints & Photographs Division/ Library of Congress, p. 7 (middle & right); Daniel Dempster Photography/ Alamy, pp. 8, 15; Alexey Stiop, pp. 8-9; AP Photo/ The Indianapolis Star, Charlie Nye/ Associated Press, pp. 10-11; Bruce MacQueen, p. 12 (left); Mayskyphoto, p. 12 (middle); Joab Souza, p. 12 (right); Mark Raycroft/ Kimball Stock, pp. 12-13; Mardis Coers Stock Connection Worldwide/ Newscom, pp. 14-15; Aaron Sprecher/ EPA/ Newscom, p. 16; Ian Dagnall/ Alamy, pp. 16-17; Owaki-Kulla/ Corbis/ Glow Images, p. 18; Bloomberg via Getty Images, p. 19; Images-USA/ Alamy, p. 20; AJ Mast/ Icon SMI 747/ Newscom, p. 21; Deb Perry/ Getty Images, p. 22 (top); Charles Brutlag, pp. 23, 29; Vitaly Korovin, p. 23 (right); WireImage/ Getty Images, p. 24; Getty Images, pp. 24-25; Dave Olive, pp. 26-27; Michael Loccisano/ Getty Images, p. 27; Pakmor, p. 28 (top); Loskutnikov, p. 28 (bottom).